From InDesign CS 5.5 to EPUB and Kindle
A Straight to the Point Miniguide

Written and illustrated by Elizabeth Castro
http://www.elizabethcastro.com/epub
Copyright © 2012 by Elizabeth Castro. All rights reserved.

Cover image modeled in Cheetah3D, Blender, and Photoshop by Andreu Cabré
http://andreucabre.blogspot.com

Published by Cookwood Press
http://www.cookwood.com

Many thanks to *Cari Jansen* and *Anne-Marie Concepción* who read through this book and offered helpful suggestions and corrections.

ISBN:

Print: 978-1-61150-020-2

EPUB: 978-1-61150-018-9

Kindle: 978-1-61150-019-6

From InDesign CS 5.5 to EPUB and Kindle

Right now there are a lot of tools on the market for creating ebooks. There is only one, however, that is useful for creating both professional-quality print books *and* ebooks. That program, of course, is Adobe InDesign. If you have a lot of existing files in InDesign or you're planning on selling both print and digital versions of your books, having a single workflow for a large part of the process can save a lot of time.

The latest version of the InDesign software, CS 5.5, has a number of improvements over earlier versions though it still has some room to grow. I'll show you how to prepare your documents for the most effective conversion to the two major ebook formats—first to EPUB for the great majority of ereaders, including iPad, iPhone, and iPod touch, and then from EPUB to Kindle/mobi for Amazon Kindle.

This is not a beginner's guide to InDesign or ebook creation. Instead, I'll be explaining how to get the most out of the new features that have been recently added to CS 5.5 that have to do with creating EPUB format ebooks, and what you need to do to convert those EPUBs into valid Kindle/mobi format books for Amazon Kindle. I will assume you have some basic knowledge of both InDesign and EPUB.

If you want more background on EPUB, I recommend my companion guide, *EPUB Straight to the Point: Creating ebooks for the Apple iPad and other ereaders*, which thoroughly covers the EPUB format itself.

Also note that there is a very important EPUB-related update to InDesign CS 5.5. To install, choose Help > Updates and follow the instructions you'll find there.

Table of Contents

InDesign to ebook in 10 steps

Going from InDesign to EPUB is a straightforward process. I'll list the steps here and then go into them in more detail in the sections that follow.

1 Learn what InDesign can and cannot do. (See "Envisioning your book" on page 7.)

2 Design your book and create a template or sample chapter with all of the styles you'll need. (See "Creating your book in InDesign" on page 17.)

3 Create your book—in one or more documents—and apply styles to format the book's contents. (See "Creating your book in InDesign" on page 17.)

4 Add any special features desired, including images, audio and video, and links, cross references and footnotes.

5 Create a table of contents style.

6 Deciding how InDesign should convert its paragraph and character styles into HTML and CSS.

7 Add pertinent metadata so that your book can be found by readers and booksellers.

8 Export the file to EPUB, taking care to choose the appropriate settings, in order to add additional metadata, create a cover, choose the desired export order, maintain image formatting, generate the CSS properly, and much more.

9 If you're not satisfied with InDesign's result, crack open the EPUB and modify the HTML and CSS by hand, for example, to prepare for conversion to Kindle/mobi or to ensure that embedded fonts are properly displayed.

10 Convert to Kindle/mobi format, if desired.

Envisioning your book

Before you begin, you should understand how print books and ebooks differ as well as InDesign's strengths and weaknesses in creating each format. In this section, I'll go over what is possible in EPUB and Kindle/mobi formats, and how much of that InDesign can do on its own.

You're probably already familiar with print books and how InDesign creates them. You create a master page with elements that should appear on each page. You then create individual pages and control the position of the text and graphics on each page. You create paragraph and character styles to control the font, size, margins, and other characteristics of the text. And when you finish, you print out pages that look precisely like what you see on screen.

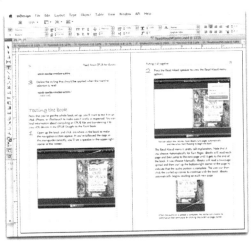

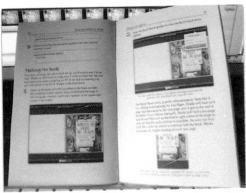

The InDesign document is identical to the printed edition.

As you probably already know, an ebook is a different kind of fish altogether. Instead of being contained in a physical page, an ebook is an amorphous stream of content that can fit into different size recipients (from iPad to Kindle Fire to iPhone) and even change sizes itself.

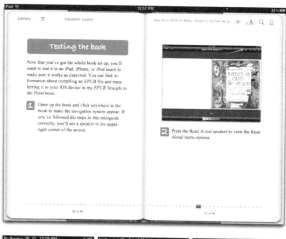

The corresponding EPUB file looks different in different ereaders, as it is reflowed, and the font-size is changed (iPad top, iPhone bottom).

This makes ebooks extremely flexible. Indeed, ebook formats are modeled after the same language—HTML—in which web pages are written and which was designed to be universally compatible with any browser on any operating system.

But that same flexibility requires the designer to give up a lot of control, particularly over positioning. No longer can you insist that a particular bit of content appear below an image (as with a caption), on page 3, or on a left hand page, or even in many cases at the top of the page. Instead, you have to be satisfied with relative control: the biggest headers should be three times as big as the body text, the image should be as wide as the page, and so on.

On the other hand, ebooks can do some things print books just cannot: contain links, audio and video, and even interactive elements.

If you want your print book and ebooks to resemble each other, you may want to study what is possible in an ebook (a moving target, but not impossible) and tailor your print book to use these characteristics, and also avoid effects that you can only achieve in print. (Of course, you may also decide to embrace the benefits of each format and allow them to diverge.)

What can you do in an ebook?

And can InDesign do it for you? Even though this section of the book couldn't possibly be current by the time you read it, most of it will be. Cutting-edge features are few. This section will give you a feel for what is generally possible in an ebook, and whether InDesign is capable of creating those effects. Also see "Converting to Kindle/mobi".

Running headers/footers

These are the lines of text that appear at the top or bottom of every page in a print book. Sometimes they change from chapter to chapter or section to section, sometimes they stay the same throughout a book. In most ereaders, the only running header or footer comes from the title of the book and is generated automatically, displayed as part of the navigational tools, and can be hidden from sight. The ebook designer cannot change the running header or footer from chapter to chapter, nor change its position or style. InDesign does not export running headers or footers, nor anything else from the Master Pages.

Page numbers

In a print book, where the number of pages is always the same, page numbers are permanently marked on each page. In an ebook whose text may be magnified or reduced in size, page numbers are variable. Some ereaders show different page numbers depending on the current size of the text and pagination of the book, some link page numbers to the page numbers in the original print book, and some offer percentages or word counts.

InDesign does not export page numbers, nor does it mark the boundaries of the print page for reference in the ebook.

Fonts

In a print book, the designer chooses one or more fonts for the text and these cannot be altered by the reader. In addition, the designer buys the font once from the font foundry and is not charged additional fees for using it in any number of copies of any number of books.

Most ereaders have a limited set of built-in fonts in which a book can be displayed. Some ereaders allow font embedding but careful attention must be paid to each font's licensing to ensure that embedding is allowed and that additional fees are not incurred. Generally, even the ereaders that allow font embedding will allow the user to override the designers' choices and revert to default fonts.

InDesign lets you choose any font that you want for both print and ebooks. Unfortunately, it doesn't embed fonts in a way that iBooks supports. I explain how to adjust the code so that iBooks can display the fonts in "Using embedded fonts in iBooks" on page 73. Kindle does not currently support font embedding at all.

Text size

In a print book, the designer chooses the size of the headers, body text, captions, and any other text in the book. These cannot be changed by the reader.

In an ebook, the designer chooses the initial size of the text, but generally the user can increase or decrease the text size. All the text is altered simultaneously so that the relative sizes stay the same. That is, if the header starts 3 times bigger than the body text, it will still be 3 times bigger than the body text even if both are reduced 25%.

InDesign exports text sizes using the font-size property. It takes the point size specified in InDesign and converts them to ems at a rate of 12 points per em. So, for 12 pt text, the CSS would be font-size: 1em. Note that Kindle discourages setting the font size for the body text.

Other text formatting

The designer can add all sorts of formatting to the text, including italics, bold, underlining, color, shadows, kerning, and more. Most of this formatting is maintained in ebooks as well and cannot be changed by the user. Some ereaders are limited with respect to how much formatting they can show. For example, black and white ereaders obviously cannot show color, but many are also unable to show kerning, shadows, or other advanced text formatting.

InDesign exports bold, italic, and bold italic styles as expected, with the font-weight and font-style properties, respectively. In CS 5.5, if desired, you can map character styles to the em or strong tags. InDesign exports underlining (specified with the underline property in the Character dialog box) using the text-decoration: underline property value pair. It exports strikethrough with text-decoration : line-through. InDesign completely ignores the options for Rule Above and Rule Below.

InDesign does export information about the color of characters, with the expected color property and a hex value for the color. It does not export information for the outline color of text.

The small caps, all caps, subscript and superscript are all properly exported: with font-variant: small-caps, text-transform: uppercase, vertical-align: super, and vertical-align: sub (and not <sup> or <sub>), respectively.

Spacing, page breaks, and orphans

In a print book, the designer chooses the amount of space between lines and paragraphs, the size of the margins, how much space should come after headers, where page breaks should or should not occur, and whether or not widows and orphans should be allowed, and to what degree.

In an ebook, some but not all of that spacing can be controlled. Line-height is always a relative value and waxes and wanes with the size of the text. InDesign calculates the ratio of the specified leading with respect to the specified font-size and uses the result as the value for line-height. For example, the CSS for 12pt text with 16pt leading would be line-height: 1.33 (16/12).

InDesign exports the values specified for Space Before, Right Indent, Space After, and Left Indent, in that order and converted to pixels, with the margin property. 1 pixel is equivalent to 1/72 of an inch, 0.35mm, 1 point, and 1/12 of a pica. So if Space Before was 6mm, Right Indent was .5in, Space After was 6pt, and Left Indent was 6px, InDesign's CSS would look like: margin: 17px 36px 6px 6px;. InDesign does not apply padding.

You can use InDesign's First Line Indent to start the first line of a paragraph either within or outside the rest of the paragraph. Negative values are allowed. InDesign converts all units to pixels (see previous paragraph) and uses the result for the value of text-indent.

InDesign has powerful settings in its Keep Options dialog box which it unfortunately does not export to EPUB. These options control page breaks, keep certain paragraphs together, and control how many lines of a paragraph can sit alone at the top or bottom of a page by themselves. Most of these features can be recreated with the CSS properties page-break-before, page-break-after, and page-break-inside, but InDesign does not yet do so. You can crack open the EPUB yourself to add them. (See "How do you crack open an EPUB?" on page 65.)

Alignment

Most professionally typeset books have justified text. It looks good thanks to the extensive kerning and tracking options, and language-specific hyphenations options offered by programs such as InDesign.

Ebooks are not so lucky. Many ereaders have rudimentary hyphenation systems, often just for the System language, and impose ereader-wide justification settings regardless of what the designer selected.

Enter InDesign. For print it offers a variety of features for controlling text alignment, from left, right, center, and justify, to justify left, justify right, justify center and full justify. Only the first four are exported to EPUB, and unfortunately, even these four are not always observed by ereaders. iBooks in particular insists on full justification by default, and hides the setting in the General Settings outside iBooks. This full justification overrides any designer-selected rules, unless you use hack the code as described in "Controlling Text Alignment" in *EPUB Straight to the Point*.

Columns

Columns make perfect sense if you have enough room for them on the printed page. With a flexible layout and the potential for a screen that's two inches wide, they can be a disaster. InDesign does not export columns.

Drop caps and all caps

A print designer often chooses to display the first letter of a chapter with a drop cap and the entire line that follows in all caps. This is also possible in ebooks.

InDesign has a nice drop cap feature that exports to EPUB by isolating the letter(s) that should be enlarged and then applies floats and margin adjustments to make them fit into the surrounding text. Unfortunately, it doesn't apply this formatting to the Drop cap style, if you've created one, but rather to a generic selector created on the fly.

Although InDesign has nested line styles that can format the first line in all caps (for example), this information is not exported to EPUB. You can adjust that by hand by cracking open the EPUB and editing the CSS.

Non-Latin characters and other symbols

A print book can contain characters from any language, in any direction, and any symbol that is required. In contrast, some ereaders are limited to only the Latin character set, and can only be set left-to-right. Others, and certainly most in the future, will be able to have text go right-to-left and vertically.

Currently InDesign exports EPUB in UTF-8 format, which means that foreign alphabets and characters are exported correctly. The only symbols that need special care are any that you've set with Zapf Dingbats.

Images

Both print books and ebooks can have images, but there is much more control over the placement of images in print books. In a print book, the designer specifies the exact location on a particular page where the image should go. In an ebook, the designer chooses the text before or after which the image should appear, but depending on the size of the text, it might be in any part of any page.

Text can wrap around images in both print and ebooks, but because some ereaders are so narrow, it is not always a feasible choice for the latter.

Finally, color images can make a print book much more expensive while they have little effect on the cost of an ebook. On the other hand, some ereaders are not capable of showing images in color.

InDesign CS5.5 offers extensive control over how you export images to EPUB. You can choose the format, size, and resolution of your images and InDesign now automatically formats wrapped text around images correctly. I'll explain the details in "Options when exporting images".

Borders and background colors

In print books, any combination of borders and background colors is possible, though the use of color can make a print book considerably more expensive to produce. In an ebook, some ereaders allow borders around text or images and background colors for pages or objects like sidebars, but support varies widely from one ereader to the next.

InDesign doesn't export any borders or background colors. If you want to use them, you have to add them manually by cracking open the EPUB and adjusting the CSS.

Table of contents and index

A print book generally has a table of contents at the beginning and an index at the end, with page number references in each. Ebooks have two kinds of tables of contents: a (required) *navigational* table of contents that appears in the menus of the ereader, and an optional, more conventional *inline* table of contents in the body of the ebook.

Ebooks can also have indexes, but instead of referring a reader to a particular page, since none exist, the index will simply link directly to the given destination. Ereaders also let readers search any phrase, whether or not it's part of an organized index.

InDesign has powerful table of contents and indexing tools for print books, but only some of that power is available for ebooks. When you export from InDesign, it will export any tables of contents that you have created, but only the first one will contain linked references. As for the index, it simply skips it altogether. I have a blog post on *Pigs, Gourds, and Wikis* that explains how to create a linked index.

Hyphenation

Print affords the designer complete control over hyphenation. Designers often adjust the spacing of lines of text or individual words to ensure that enough but not too much hyphenation is used and that the words in the rest of the paragraph have the proper spacing. There are very distinct rules of hyphenation for different languages.

For some unknown reason, ereaders don't yet allow the same level of control over hyphenation. First, I have yet to see an ereader that can distinguish between two different languages in a single ebook, or even one that pays attention to settings in the EPUB when using more than one language. iBooks even gets hyphenation wrong in English on an English system (though it mostly gets it right). But there's no guarantee for multilingual documents. Kindle has no hyphenation at all.

A designer can choose to disallow hyphenation completely (for example, in a header) or to depend on the vagaries of each ereader in which the ebook is displayed.

InDesign supports hyphenation to the nth degree, but unfortunately does not export that information to EPUB. You can, however, edit the EPUB files to exert some control over hyphenation yourself, for those ereaders that support it.

Links

In a print book, it's common to refer a reader to another page with "see page 245" or "consult Chapter 3, *Working with images*", or even "check her website: http://www.elizabethcastro.com". In an ebook, since page numbers don't exist, it makes more sense to create hyperlinks to specific sections of a book.

InDesign helps you create *hyperlinks*, in which you have to designate both the text for the link as well as its destination—which might be inside the book or outside on a website—*cross references*, in which the text for the link comes directly from the text in the destination, and *footnotes*, that link to a source or other information about the text.

InDesign exports links to EPUB (and thus to Kindle/mobi), as expected. A bug in InDesign CS 5 in which some links were broken has thankfully been fixed in InDesign CS 5.5.

Tables

Tables are a key ingredient to many print books but in ebooks they suffer from the same issue as columns and text wrap: there is often simply not enough room for them on the screen. A table's rigidity is its downfall since it can't adapt to smaller areas or smaller screens. Some ereaders let you display tables full screen but others break them up or squash them into the screen. InDesign creates tables very well, and exports them with standard HTML code, but doesn't do anything special to help adapt them to smaller screens.

Audio and video

There are some print books with audio and video add-ons—a book with bird calls comes to mind—but they require an additional device to make them work. Ebooks can have audio and video incorporated into the page, but not all ereaders can handle them. It's a good idea to have fallback solutions in those ebooks in which audio and video fail. You can now export audio and video from InDesign to EPUB. See "Placing and exporting audio and video" on page 35 for details and caveats.

Currently, only Apple allows independent publishers to add audio and video to their ebooks. For awhile it looked like Amazon supported embedded audio and video as well, though only in Kindle apps on iOS (!), but now they don't even allow that. Barnes & Noble's NOOK Color supports audio and video but won't accept such files submitted by independent publishers.

Creating your book in InDesign

Once you know what you can do with InDesign, you can prepare the design of your book. I generally do this step by placing a sample chapter in an InDesign document of the proper size for the print edition, and then by defining paragraph, character, and object styles.

It's fine to include features that only work in print or only work in digital, as long as you're aware that they'll only work in one or the other formats. For example, it's perfectly reasonable to create master pages and master page items, say for running heads or page numbers for the print edition, just as long as you keep in mind that they will not appear in the EPUB or Kindle/mobi editions of your book.

Apart from the actual appearance of your book—which will be defined by the styles that you create—you should also decide whether to create a single document for your entire book or to divide your book into multiple documents, perhaps for individual chapters. Either way is fine. While earlier versions of InDesign favored one system or another, I think it's safe to say that you can now choose the system that is most comfortable for you, and it won't greatly affect the ebook versions of your work. That said, unless your book is extremely small, I recommend creating an InDesign book to organize the contents into multiple documents. InDesign books are handy when working with very large books as they let you work with smaller, more agile chapters. It's also true that some numbering and section options are only available when you have separate documents. Finally separate InDesign documents always start on a new page in an ebook. This is still the only foolproof method for creating a page break.

To create a book, choose File > New > Book, give the book a file name and then click the plus sign in the new Book panel to add chapters to your book.

It's important to designate a Style Source for your book by clicking to the left of the ID icon and chapter name in the Book panel. The Style Source is the chapter that is used to generate the table of contents, and its styles are the ones copied to the rest of your book when you choose Synchronize Book in the Book panel menu.

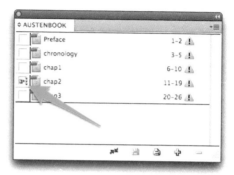

The document with the little icon filled in to the left indicates which file is the Style Source for your book.

Creating a template

A template is nothing more than a sample chapter that includes all of the styles that you will need throughout your book. If you created a sample chapter while designing your book, that file may work fine as a template. You can always add to a template as you progress through the book, since sometimes it's not until later that you realize you need a new style for a particular situation.

Saving a template

You can save a template in a special format to keep from making changes to it inadvertently by going to File > Save As and choosing InDesign Template in the Format menu. That said, if, like me, you find you're constantly updating your template, it can be easier to treat one of the live chapters of your book as the template. Then you can add styles to the chapter, and simply re-import the styles to the rest of your book's chapters.

To import styles from one document to another, choose Load Paragraph Styles from the Paragraph Styles panel menu and then choose the template chapter that contains the desired styles.

To import styles from a template chapter into *all* of the other chapters of the book, open the Book panel, and make sure the template chapter is specified as the Style Source for your book.

Then choose Synchronize Book from the Books panel menu. As long as the appropriate options are chosen in the Synchronize Options dialog box, the styles from the Style Source document will be copied to all of the other documents in your book.

The importance of styles

Styles are the key to formatting both print and ebooks in InDesign. Styles let you tag an entire collection of content and format it in one fell swoop. In addition, styles in InDesign are almost analogous with styles in EPUB, so by applying styles in InDesign you make it easier to control and format your ebooks as well.

All major ebook formats are based on HTML, the same language that web pages are written in. HTML is an ingenious system of *marking* (that's the *M* in HTML) different parts of your content to identify what each one is. So a <p> tag might identify a paragraph and an <h1> tag might identify a top level heading. If you're used to working with InDesign, you may think this looks very familiar to styles, and you'd be right.

There are some slight differences. In InDesign you define styles for paragraphs, characters, and even objects, by specifying the formatting that should be applied to each one. In HTML, you first specify what kind of content something is (a paragraph, a division, an image, etc.), then you identify particular instances of those elements (say, all of the "bodytext" paragraphs, or perhaps all of the "photo" images), and finally, in an accompanying style sheet, you define the formatting that should be applied to those elements.

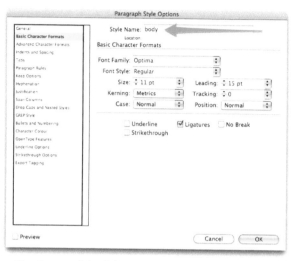

Here's some of the definition of the body *style in InDesign.*

When InDesign exports a file to EPUB, it creates p elements with the name of the style of each paragraph as a class, by default. In CS 5.5, you can customize how paragraph and character styles are converted to HTML and CSS. I'll show you how in "Mapping tags to export" on page 44.

```
121  ▼  p.body {
122         font-family : Optima, sans-serif;
123         font-weight : normal;
124         font-style : normal;
125         font-size : 0.92em;
126         text-decoration : none;
127         font-variant : normal;
128         line-height : 1.36;
129         text-align : left;
130         color : #000000;
131         text-indent : 0px;
132         margin : 0px 0px 6px 0px;
133  ⌐  }
```

InDesign converts the style definition of the body *style into a CSS selector applied to* p *elements with class* body.

The way in which you apply styles depends a bit on where the content comes from originally. If you're importing documents that already contain formatting, you'll want to maintain as much of that as is useful. If you import plain text documents, I recommend applying a body style to the entire document at once, and then applying styles to the headers, captions, images, and other special elements individually.

Creating a cover

One of InDesign CS 5.5's most notable improvements is that you can now associate a cover with the exported EPUB. And although you generate the file during the actual export process, it's a good idea to prepare the content of your cover ahead of time.

InDesign can either generate a cover image from the contents of the first page of your book or document, or you can link to an external image that you've prepared elsewhere, perhaps in Photoshop. Let's look at the first system.

Generating a cover from the first page

One of the advantages of creating a cover right in your InDesign document is that it will automatically have the same proportions as your ebook. This is not required, but it probably makes sense. Note that cover images do not all have to be a standard size. On iBooks, they must be at least 600 pixels wide along the larger axis. On a Nook, I recommend 600 x 800px. Kindle requires that the dimensions be at least 500 x 800 pixels and recommends a height/width ratio of 1.6.

1 Place the images and text that should be included in your cover on the first page of your first InDesign document.

Remember that the cover of an ebook is rarely displayed full size. More often, only a tiny representation of it is shown, either on an ebook commerce site like Amazon or Apple's iBookstore or in the bookshelf on an ereader. So, it's important to make sure that your cover works at a small size. To that end, you can adjust the cover so that extraneous text and images are removed and that the title and author are a bit bigger than might be warranted in print.

This cover is made up of a background image and two text frames.

You could stop here and just use the Export options that I'll explain later to generate your cover. The problem is that while InDesign will create a *cover image* for you from the first page of your book, it will only use that image in iBooks opposite the table of contents and as an icon in the iBookstore. However it won't use it as the first page of your book. Instead, it will output the contents of the page individually: first the two text frames, then the image. The special font that I've used here will either require special treatment, or be ignored altogether.

The first page of your book does not look like the original cover.

The solution is to group the individual pieces of your book and then have InDesign rasterize them (convert them to a single image) both for the cover and for the first page.

2   Select all the parts of the cover and choose Object > Group. You will see a dotted line around the image and the text frames.

3   Next, choose Object > Object Export Options. In the dialog box that appears, choose the EPUB and HTML tab. Then check Custom Rasterization, Custom Image Alignment and Spacing, and Insert Page Break (After Image). (For help choosing a Size and Resolution, see "Options when exporting images" on page 54.)

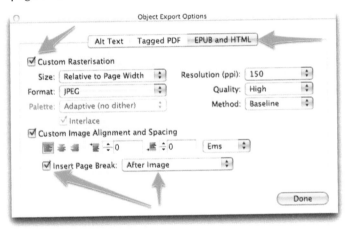

These options will make InDesign create a single image file out of your image and text. Normally, Apple won't permit you to include text in an image, but it's OK and even expected for a cover. When you check the Insert Page Break (After Image) option, you ensure that the cover image will be placed on its own page. Don't create a page break before the image, as that would generate a blank page at the beginning of your book.

4   Finally, click Done.

Now your first page will work as both the cover image and the first page of your book once you are ready to Export to EPUB (and later to Kindle/mobi) as described in "Exporting to EPUB".

Note: I have noticed that InDesign sometimes adds extra white space around images that have been cropped or large text blocks. You may need to adjust accordingly.

Placing images and controlling export order

InDesign CS 5.5 gives you three choices about how to control the order of the elements on the printed page when converted into an ebook. I'm only going to talk about the first and last, Based on Page Layout and Based on Articles Panel. For more info on using XML with InDesign, I recommend reading Cari Jansen's blog post: http://carijansen.com/2010/09/18/moving-print-publications-to-epub/

InDesign's default method of exporting content is to begin at the left-most, topmost frame on the first page, export its *entire* contents—regardless of how many frames or pages it appears on—and then continue on with the next item down until it reaches the bottom of the page. It then continues with the next left most object. For very simple layouts, like novels, this may work just fine. For more complicated layouts, you may be surprised at how the exported EPUB is ordered. For long passages of text with intermittent graphic elements, your best option for controlling the order of the contents in an ebook is with anchored objects—either inline or custom positioned.

The new system of Articles InDesign CS 5.5 offers an additional alternative for controlling export order. You can assign text frames and images to an article and then reorder the elements within an article, as well as rearrange the articles themselves, until you're satisfied with the export order. This can be very useful when you have short text frames, but it doesn't help with placing images in specific locations in a long block of text.

Using inline objects to control export order

If your layout is relatively simple, but with long bits of text, the best way to control the order in which images or other elements appear in your exported ebook is by placing them right into the flow of the text in your InDesign document. If you place them after a given paragraph in your print book, that's where they'll appear in the ebook as well.

(Note that I will be talking about images in this section, but you can use most of these techniques for independent text frames—like pull quotes—as well.)

Let's look at a quick example. Here is a very simply laid out book. The image is placed in an independent graphic frame.

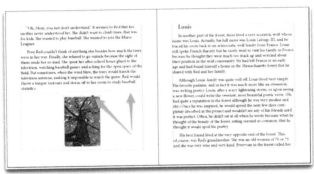

The solid blue box at the right end of the top edge indicates that the image is in an independent graphic frame. Notice how the text frame does not contain the graphic.

When we export this book with the "Based on Page Layout" option, InDesign exports all the text in the entire story, and then places the image at the end. That's not what we want. What we want is for that tree image to always appear just after the paragraph in the story about the trees. The solution is to create an inline image—the simplest kind of anchored object—that flows with the text and whose content is exported together with the text.

I like to create a special format for the paragraph that will contain the inline image, both so I can adjust the leading in my print book as well as adjust the formatting in the resulting ebook.

1   Create a style for inline elements. I call mine "illustration". Be sure that the illustration's style's leading is set to Auto so that the paragraph expands with the height of the illustration. You can also adjust the Space Before and Space After fields as desired.

2   Place the cursor where you want to insert your image. Press Return, then use the up arrow to return to your new paragraph and style it with your illustration style.

3   Choose File > Place and select the image that you wish to place in your book.

You can resize, crop, rotate, add space around, or otherwise modify the image as desired. Upon export, you can tell InDesign to maintain these changes for the EPUB document, or to ignore them. (See "Options when exporting images" on page 54 for details.)

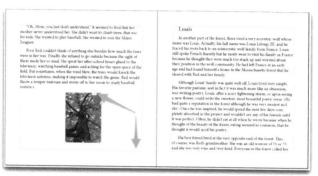

An inline graphic displays an anchor symbol when you select it.
Note also that the text frame encloses the inline graphic.

This time, when you export this document to EPUB, the image will appear after the same paragraph that it followed in your InDesign document.

If you're converting a print book into ebook format and already have all of the images placed, you can quickly slide an image inline by selecting it, holding down the Shift key, and dragging the blue square in the upper right corner to the desired location in the text.

Custom positioned anchored objects

Inline anchored objects don't give you much control over their placement in the print edition of your book. They flow along as if they were just one more paragraph of text. If you're interested in wrapping text around objects, or if the objects are already placed and you simply want to control where they appear in your exported text, I recommend using what InDesign calls *custom positioned anchored objects*. InDesign CS 5.5 makes it really easy to create a custom positioned anchored object from an existing object—placed practically anywhere on the page—and to link it to the bit of text that it should appear next to upon export.

For this example, imagine that we start with a text frame that has an independent image sitting on top of it with text wrap applied.

1   Click the image to select it and view the anchor box on the top right corner.

The solid blue box at the right end of the top edge indicates that the image is not anchored.

2   Drag the blue anchor box to the spot in the text where you wish it to appear when exported to EPUB. We'll drag it right before the first word in the paragraph.

Drag the solid blue box to the beginning of the paragraph that should flow around it.

The image's position on the page does not change, but now the blue box turns into a blue anchor to show that the image is anchored in the text and will be exported at the point in the text where it is anchored. If it has text wrap applied as in this example, the text wrap will also be maintained in the EPUB file.

The solid blue box at the right end of the top edge indicates that the image is not anchored.

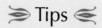

Tips

Note that you can't anchor an image with text wrapped around it to a spot that's *after* the location of the image itself. If you do, the text wrap is eliminated.

If you hold down the Shift key while you drag the blue box, the image is automatically converted to an inline object and placed at the insertion point.

When we export to EPUB, the image is where we want it—embedded in the text.

An anchored image around which text is flowed will be exported as a floating image in the EPUB file. Unfortunately, the space around it is not maintained.

If you want to add a little space around the image, you can go into the EPUB file and adjust the CSS, or as long as you choose Preserve Appearance from Layout when you export to EPUB, you can adjust the spacing in InDesign, and the space will be preserved.

Using articles to control export order

With InDesign CS 5.5, you have an added tool in your toolbox for controlling the order of exported items, the Articles panel. An article is a named collection of one or more text frames, images, or other objects. Your document can have multiple articles. Once you've defined your articles, you can set the export order of the contents of an ebook by rearranging the elements in an article or by rearranging the articles themselves. It can be very helpful.

Note, however, that articles can only control the order of *entire* text threads, images, or other objects. You can't specify that a given image be exported after a particular position in an accompanying story. It must either go before the whole story or after the whole story. In addition, if you have inline images or sidebars—anchored within a story, as described in the previous sections—you won't be able to change the order of those objects in the Articles panel. They will always be exported with the text in which they appear. For more granular control, see the previous sections on "Using inline objects to control export order" and "Custom positioned anchored objects" .

Here is a book of articles about crazy weather. Notice how there are six frames on the page, two photos and four text articles.

If you export this document to InDesign with the default "Based on Page Layout" option, you may be surprised and probably disappointed at how things are ordered in the resulting EPUB.

First we see the body of the text, since it is the left most item in the layout in InDesign:

The body of the text is exported first since it was the left-most item.

Next, we see the rest of the stories output in left to right order:

This is not how we want the content ordered in the ebook.

For this example, let's say that we want the larger right hand image to come first, followed by the headline, the body of the article, and then the author byline. We want to eliminate "New England News" from the export entirely. And we really want the smaller image to be embedded in the text itself.

1 The first step is to open the Articles panel by choosing Window > Articles.

The Articles panel starts out empty. You have to add articles to it manually either by dragging frames to it or by clicking the plus sign.

You can either drag individual frames, stories, or images to the Articles panel or Command-click (Control-click on PC) to add all of the elements on the current page to the Articles panel.

Note that an article is not equivalent to a text frame or an image, but is more like a folder that can contain a series of text threads or images.

2 Command-click the plus sign in the Articles panel to add all of the elements on the page to a single article in the Articles panel, or Shift-click each article individually before clicking the plus sign to add them in the order they were selected. (Thanks @carijansen!).

3 In the Article Options box that appears, give the article a name and check the Include When Exporting box.

The name that you choose for the article is used as the class name for the div *in the exported EPUB file.*

The stories are added to a single article in the Articles panel. Notice that when you select an element, for example, the image in the upper right of the screen, a blue square appears next to that image in the Articles panel.

Each one of the elements on the page is listed in the Snowtober article in the Articles panel.

4   Now that the elements are listed, we can order them as we wish, simply by dragging. We want the larger image first, followed by the title and the author's byline, followed by the body text.

You can reorder the elements in the Articles panel without affecting how they are displayed on the page.

Eliminate items from the article that you don't want to include in the EPUB file by selecting them and clicking the trash can. We'll eliminate the New England News header.

Eliminate individual stories from the export by selecting them and clicking the garbage can. You can keep an entire article from being included by unchecking its name.

 Export the document to EPUB being careful to choose Same as Articles panel under Ordering in the General tab of the EPUB Export Options dialog box.

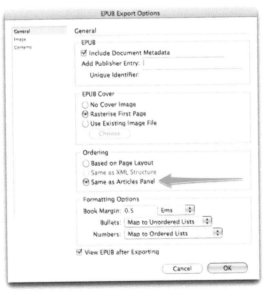

Don't forget to choose Same as Articles panel in the EPUB Export Options dialog box.

Now when you export this document to EPUB, the order is much closer to what we want. (I'll go over Export options in more detail in "Exporting to EPUB" on page 49.)

Now the stories in the InDesign document are exported the way we want, and the header is not included.

Tips

It's important to note that once you anchor an image to a specific location in a body of text, you can't change its export order in the Articles panel—indeed it won't even appear in the Articles panel. It becomes a part of the text item and is exported together with that text.

Or, put another way, you can only reorder independent text items and images.

Placing and exporting audio and video

With version 5.5 of InDesign comes the ability to export any placed audio or video files into an EPUB document.

You can place an audio or video file in the usual way (File > Place) or by opening the Media panel and clicking the little filmstrip in the bottom right corner. InDesign currently supports .mp3 and .mp4 media files only. Once the media file is placed (and still selected), you can set options for it in that same Media panel.

Click the film at the bottom-right to place a video or audio file.

Check the Play on Page Load box to have the media file play automatically when the reader gets to the page that contains it. Earlier versions of iBooks did not allow audio or video to play automatically, but from at least version 1.3.2 on, it does. Note however, that iBooks is not very consistent about when it plays an audio file. Sometimes it plays automatically when you open the book, sometimes when you get to the page that contains the audio. Whether you choose Stop on Page Turn or not, iBooks does not currently stop the audio unless you press the pause button.

Check the Loop box to have the media file repeat from the beginning each time it reaches the end.

For video, don't forget to choose (any!) option for Controller so that InDesign includes the controls and your readers can turn your video on and off.

If you've placed a video, you *should* be able to choose an image from the video as the poster, or still image, that identifies your video when the video is paused. However, while this works inside InDesign, InDesign 5.5 forgets to add the code to the HTML file and so it does not appear in the EPUB file. One workaround is to simply add the poster image by hand yourself. InDesign similarly lets you designate a poster for an audio file but does not export that to EPUB either.

And finally, note that while InDesign CS 5.5 automatically adds play and pause controls to audio files, it does not do so for video. I recommend choosing an option in the Controller menu for a video file (any option will do) so that InDesign adds controls="controls" to the HTML which will cause the Play, Airplay, and Full screen icons to appear on the video file, giving your user some control over when the video plays (or stops playing).

Note that while you can wrap text around your video or audio files, InDesign won't export the space around it. To adjust the space around audio and video files, you'll have to edit your CSS by hand.

Creating links

One of the nice advantages an ebook has over its print counterpart is the ability to fly from one spot in the book to another without having to leaf through to find a specific page. While you can also create links to outside resources (say, a link on a website), these require opening an external application like a web browser and some ebookstores frown on them in general, considering them possible competition! At any rate, I'll focus on links within an ebook from one section to another.

InDesign creates three kinds of intrabook links: hyperlinks, cross references, and footnotes. A hyperlink connects the origin to a marked destination with any text you like. A cross-reference uses the text from the destination as the clickable text—and InDesign will update it if you change the text. A footnote has an automatically-numbered reference that links to the content of the footnote.

Earlier versions of InDesign had a terrible bug that didn't properly generate links in multi-document EPUBs. Thankfully, that issue has been fixed in InDesign CS 5.5 and you can now have a book with several chapters and correctly link between one chapter and the next—or the previous!

Creating hyperlinks

To create a hyperlink, you have to mark the destination first, and then go to where you want the link to appear, and create a hyperlink there.

1 Navigate to the location in your book where the destination of the link should be. Select the bit of text that should appear when the reader clicks the link.

2 Choose Window > Interactive > Hyperlinks to display the Hyperlinks panel if it is not already visible.

3 Choose New Hyperlink Destination from the Hyperlinks panel menu. The selected text appears in the New Hyperlink Destination dialog box.

4 Choose Text Anchor if it's not already selected. You can change the name of the hyperlink if you like, especially if it's very long. (The selected text won't be affected.)

5 Click OK.

It's fine to abbreviate or change the Name of the hyperlink destination to make it easier to remember.

6 Next, navigate to the place in your book where you want to create the link. Select the text that will be highlighted as a link, the "clickable" text.

7 This time, choose New Hyperlink in the Hyperlinks Panel menu. In the New Hyperlink box that appears, choose Text Anchor from the Link To box at the top and then choose the desired destination in the Text Anchor box. (This should match what you had in step 5.)

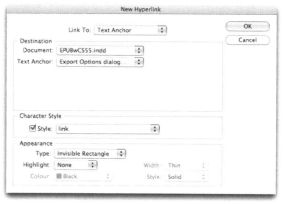

You can link to destinations in other documents in your book by choosing them in the Document menu.

8 If desired, check the Style box and select the character style that should be applied to the hyperlink.

Creating cross references

Cross references are really great when you want to reference the name or number of a particular section or chapter of your book. You can have InDesign keep track of what that section was called or how that chapter was numbered and update it automatically. For example, you could create a reference like *see Chapter 1 for details*. And if the destination that you choose happens to end up being Chapter 2, the cross reference will automatically change to *see Chapter 2 for details*.

1 To create a cross reference, it's important to make sure that you've styled your destination text properly, particularly with the desired paragraph style.

2 Choose Window > Interactive > Hyperlinks if the Hyperlinks panel is not already showing.

3 Place the cursor where you want the cross-reference to appear. Remember that you will be pulling in text from the destination, and thus if you have anything already selected, it will be replaced with the incoming text.

4 Choose Insert Cross-Reference from the Hyperlinks flyaway menu.

5 In the dialog box that appears, choose either Paragraph or Text Anchor in the Link to box. If you choose Text Anchor, you can reference any hyperlink destination (as created in previous section). If you choose Paragraph, you can reference any styled paragraph.

6 If you've chosen Paragraph, next you'll choose the paragraph style and then the actual paragraph that you want to reference. If you've chosen Text Anchor, you'll now select the one that you want to use. Remember that the name of the Text Anchor sometimes matches its contents, but is not required to do so.

Next choose the Format for the cross-reference. You can decide to use the entire contents of the selected paragraph, or just the number, and you can add text or styling.

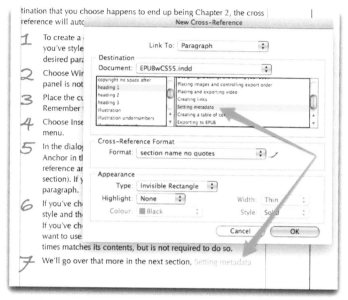

In this example, the Format uses the full text of the paragraph as the cross reference text. You can see what it will look like in the text.

Thankfully, the Appearance Type now seems to have a default value of Invisible Rectangle, which is what I recommend.

8 Click OK to complete the cross-reference.

Creating footnotes

Another kind of link that can be very handy in an ebook is footnotes. InDesign can create and lay out footnotes at the bottom of your print pages, and then collect them at the end of a chapter or the end of the book for the digital version.

1 To create a footnote in your book, choose Type > Insert Footnote. The cursor is automatically placed in the space for footnotes which in turn is automatically created at the bottom of the text frame and a numbered superscript appears at the end of the text.

It seems there is justification for being a helicopter grandparent with these kinds of issues. The question is: what do we do about it? At the risk of yielding to foot-in-the-mouth disease, when do we say "I'm worried?"

Hovering is acceptable behavior for grandparents as long as it doesn't become obsessive. "Pick your battles," says family psychologist Dr. R.C. Dubuc. "If you've developed the reputation of worrying about every minor concern, you won't be taken seriously for the big events."

Patience is difficult to manage, but if practiced, it pays off. Wait until your grandchild's parent asks for advice. You may wait forever, but miracles occasionally happen. In the meantime, let them know you're there to be a sounding board.

Grandparents are important in a child's life by offering stability and unconditional love. They can also influence children by being a good role model. Spending quality time, without anything being plugged in, sets a good example.

20. WHEN IS NAKED OKAY?

U nlike a spunky young man last summer who was severely reprimanded for being naked when he was going through a drive-through fast food chain, our small, adorable grandchildren are allowed to be naked. Aren't they?

Opinions differ certainly regarding the appropriateness of nudity among children and certainly age plays a part as well. Few of us flinch when a toddler streaks naked across a room. We might raise an eyebrow if the same child were 10. Some of us feel our sensibilities have been insulted. Others appreciate the freedom and innocence of children. We may even feel envy, especially in a summer heat wave.

When my children were young and took off their pajamas in their bedrooms before announcing their presence to the adult world and streaking into our living room, my mother would shriek in surprise. She was never angry, but made it clear by her comments to my children that they were *naked* and it wasn't appropriate. As a result, they repeated the behavior every time she came to visit.

"Children see no stigma when it comes to nudity," says family psychologist Dr. R.C. Dubuc. "In fact, it doesn't take them long to learn that streaking is a way of getting attention from adults."

Parents set the rules for behavior, including nudity and they should be clear, consistent and respected by all caregivers, including grandparents. Appropriate behavior varies from family to family of course, and attitudes may be more relaxed in your home than in that of your children or vice versa. What's important is to find out the rules the parents adhere to and to abide by them.

There are other issues, of course, that present touchy subjects for parents and grandparents. While it's normal (and in no way sexually related) for small children, under the age of three, to discover and touch their private parts, it's often a habit that makes adults feel uncomfortable. Even though the touching is more of a soothing motion, like twirling a lock of hair, children don't associate touching with sexuality until they are older. Until the teen years, children's interest in sexuality is mostly curiosity.

Most experts agree that these behaviors such as running naked or touching private parts should be ignored at first. Most children who are ignored will stop the habit. Some may use both as a way to get attention, especially if there's a substantial reaction from an adult. "Becoming too emotional may blow the situation out of proportion," says Dr. Dubuc.

Different cultures have different attitudes to child nudity. In Europe, a naked child on a public beach is a common sight. In North America, depending on the region and the age of the child, it may be less common. Whether or not we're comfortable with our naked grandchildren, we need to be respectful of the sensibilities of others in public places.

21 . DO GRANDKIDS BELONG IN RESTAURANTS?

Recently, two restaurants in the U.S. made headlines with new policies regarding children. One restaurant has simply banned children under the age of six completely from that fine dining establishment. The other has made it clear that the management "will not tolerate" families with noisy, screaming children disturbing the dining experience of others.

Am I just old and cranky with a fading memory, but aren't children noisier and more annoying now in restaurants than they were when I was taking my perfect children out to dine? And let's add airplanes here too, where the child sitting behind kicks the back of my seat for the entire transatlantic flight, sitting with parents who seem to be completely oblivious to my discomfort.

As much as I adore children, I applaud at *least* the restaurant in the U.S. who will not tolerate screaming children who disturb other diners. It may be maternally incorrect to applaud this new policy, but since a recent survey indicated that 60 per cent of travelers would like a separate area for families with children on planes, I have a feeling I am not alone in suggesting that there should be rules for children's behavior on planes *and* in restaurants.

Weren't we all chastised to sit up straight, chew with our mouths closed and stay at the table until everyone has finished eating? Didn't we raise our children to follow the same set of good manners?

Perhaps it's a loss of courtesy in this generation of young parents, but it seems there's an attitude that just because they have spawned these miracle offspring makes them immune to consideration for others. It seems these parents regard restaurants, airplane aisles and grocery stores extended adventure playgrounds. I think the operative phrase these days is 'sense of entitlement.' That's a kind phrase for just plain rude!

There's a plethora of family-style and fast-food restaurants where children are welcome and catered to with indoor playgrounds, coloring books and crayons. My stand is that if parents insist on bringing their children to a restaurant that fits more aptly into the fine-dining category, they need to insist their children exhibit appropriate and considerate behavior and manners.

We don't expect diners to suffer from secondhand smoke. We expect pet owners to keep dogs on a leash and pick up after them. We wouldn't tolerate disorderly behavior from an adult in a restaurant. Why can't we expect the same courtesies from parents with disorderly children?

How do other grandparents feel? Christine takes her grandchildren out for restaurant meals frequently. "With my grandkids under the age of 10, I take them to a kids' restaurant," she says. They have a limited attention span and a limited palate, so why fight it? But once they're teens and can appreciate the pleasure of fine dining, I will take them to fancier places."

Martin adores his grandchildren, "but when I go out for dinner with my wife, I frankly want a quiet dinner with a good bottle of wine. That is not the atmosphere for my grandkids, and to be honest, I don't appreciate other diners bringing noisy children either."

George and Marie have been taking their children and grandchildren to their upscale golf club every Sunday for dinner since the grandchildren were toddlers. "But, the parents bring crafts to keep them busy while we wait for dinner," he explains, "and the kids are all really well behaved. Their parents make sure of it. So I would be very offended if my club suddenly banned children."

While living in Europe 30 years ago when my children were young, we dined out a lot like other Europeans. Maybe they've just been civilized longer, but Europeans seem to have the solution for family dining. There were usually children's playgrounds as part of the restaurant, or often someone would come out from the kitchen and take one of our children back in with them so we could enjoy our meal.

There may not be a solution in North America that pleases everyone, unless restaurants close off 'family-friendly' sections behind a soundproof glass partition, similar to the smoking section partitions of yore.

Apparently, the U.S. restaurant refusing to tolerate screaming children has seen a drop in families frequenting the North Carolina establishment, but actually has enjoyed a significant boost in clientele numbers in general. Isn't that interesting?

22.WHEN OUR CHILDREN ADOPT

More than 60 years ago, when my uncle and aunt told my grandparents they were thinking of adopting a child, my grandfather's response was, "Why would you want to raise a child that isn't your own?" It wasn't a question; it was a judgment. As a result, my uncle and aunt gave up the idea. Without the support of grandparents, they lost their enthusiasm for the plan. Unfortunately, they missed the opportunity of being parents, but we, their nieces and nephews, benefitted because they showered us with all that unspent parental affection and attention.

Adoption practices have changed considerably since then. In my grandparents' time, adoption was a secretive process, where little was known about the child's background and/or the identity of the child's birth parents was inaccessible. In many cases, there was also a stigma of shame, first that the adopting couple, in many cases were infertile; secondly the child being adopted was often the result of a young, unmarried girl who went 'away' to have the baby. Some children were not even told they had been adopted until later in their lives, if at all.

Today, the stigma of secrecy and shame is gone. Young parents are adopting openly and enthusiastically. And many are adopting children from other countries and other ethnic groups. In most cases, information about the child's ancestry, identity and culture is freely shared.

Still, for many grandparents, accepting the idea of adoption may be difficult. While the adopting parents have had time to process the idea and have investigated the various options, grandparents need their own time as well to adjust to a situation that is new and unfamiliar.

"When our daughter and her husband told us they had already begun the process of adopting a little girl from China, it took Charlie and I time to digest the news," says Leona . "I have to admit we probably didn't receive the news with the enthusiasm our daughter expected, but we just needed time to readjust our feelings."

Since then, Leona and Charlie have been educating themselves about international adoption and have been reading about China. "We certainly wanted to be part of the process and show our children that we will support their decision and welcome our new granddaughter," says Charlie. "We had lots of discussions with our grown kids about our new role, and now, we're all on the same page. We explained to them that we needed to educate ourselves so we could be prepared. Now, we're just as excited as they are."

Being part of the intricacies of the adoption process may not be possible for grandparents. They won't be involved in the paperwork, but that doesn't mean they can't be part of the anticipation and share in the preparation for the new child's arrival. While some of the details while waiting for a child to arrive through the adoption process may be different, many of the same customs *can* be celebrated, such as baby showers and buying equipment for the new child.

Nora was delighted when her friends and neighbors hosted a shower for the new grand-daughter her son and daughter-in-law adopted. "I had been to many of the showers for grandchildren of my friends, so they wanted to reciprocate," she says. "I didn't expect a shower, but it was a lovely gesture that showed the support of my friends."

Nora offers advice to grandparents of children adopted from other racial groups. "I didn't expect to be asked questions about Nuala's ethnic background," she says, "so I was taken aback the first time a neighbor made comments about her skin color. Fortunately, in my family, we had all made a decision to be open and very proud of Nuala's heritage, so I was able to answer my neighbor's questions. Still, it's important to have a discussion with family early on, so everyone has the same guidelines regarding privacy."

There are many other ways of supporting the adoptive couple, especially those considering a child from another country. You can offer air miles for travel to the country for instance. Discussing current events from a child's birth country and simply listening to your adult child's feelings as she or he go through this challenging process will demonstrate your love and support. And of course, practical help such as an offer to babysit will ensure you're a welcome and connected grandparent.

23.WHEN OUR CHILDREN DIVORCE

When Alice's daughter and son-in-law divorced in the mid-80s, she was devastated. "I adored my son-in-law," she says. "With three daughters, he had become the son we hadn't had." Fortunately, the divorce was amicable and Alice sees her son-in-law at family gatherings such as the grandkids' graduations and her grand-daughter's wedding last summer. "But I grieved for a long time," she says, "and, to be honest, I was really angry with my daughter, for a while, for not trying harder.

For people like Alice, a divorce can foster resentment, especially if the partner left behind is her child. It can also be distressing if the partner, who has left, has taken the grandchildren, leaving a grandparent with the possibility of limited or even no access to the children.

Even when it's an amicable separation, divorce is painful for the partners, and it can be more distressing and bewildering for children, who may even feel responsible and suffer from guilt and depression. The very same emotions can plague grandparents.

Grief, the kind Alice felt, is a common emotion for people who have had a good relationship with a daughter-in-law or son-in-law. Grief is a natural reaction and will take time to heal. There may also be guilt over divided loyalties, especially if it's your child who has done the leaving.

For a divorced grandparent, there may be an added burden of guilt that they are responsible by example for the failure of a child's relationship.

"Even those whose marriages have lasted may feel they could have done something to encourage a child's marriage and avert a family disaster," says family psychologist Dr. R.C. Dubuc. All of these feelings take time to work through, but the best solution is to steer our energies in a more positive direction and be (quietly) supportive."

Being supportive to grandchildren is an important priority. Children of parents going through a separation or divorce may feel confused, sad, even angry. They're caught between two people they love. At this time, they need a sounding board, someone they trust to listen to their frustrations and their fears, someone to make them feel safe.

That role may be a difficult one for a grandparent, who undoubtedly has his own feelings of fear, grief and divided loyalties. The challenge is to be the sounding board and to refrain from laying blame on either parent. Children need reassurance that they didn't cause the breakup. More than anything, they need the stability of a warm relationship they can count on and where they feel safe.

Ben had their grandchildren move in with them for four weeks while their son and daughter-in-law worked through custody issues, financial arrangements and the division of property. "It was a challenging time for us," Ben says. "We had to work hard to separate our feelings and set them aside to reassure the children and provide them with a sense that they wouldn't be deserted." While it was difficult for Ben and Elizabeth, this time-out for their grandchildren gave them a sense of security and a safe place with people they knew were "on their side."

Grandparents may not be able to put the family back together the way it was, but they can play a role in providing stability and helping the family, particularly the children, in their transition to a new family structure.

24. YOURS, MINE OR OURS?

Many of us who have embarked on second (or third) marriages have inherited new families, including new grandchildren. How do we balance the relationship with our spouse while being a contributing grandparent? And to complicate matters further, how do we balance the time and effort spent with our own grandchildren with those who came in the package with a new spouse.

George and Celeste bring 10 grandchildren to their relationship. George has three grandchildren and Celeste has seven. They winter in Mexico and spend summers at the cottage. How do they divide their time and effort with their grandchildren? "We each take the responsibility for our own individual grandchildren," says George. "If Celeste's kids need babysitting, she goes and I stay at the cottage." It works for Celeste who says "When I am babysitting, I am focused on the kids, so it's better if I'm there on my own without worrying about whether George is bored or uncomfortable."

Negotiations become more complicated when their kids and grandkids all want to come to the cottage at the same time. Who gets first dibs? What's fair? "We have lots of room, but basically, we tell them that the first ones who ask to come get priority," says George. "If they all come at once, that's fine too, but they have to take whatever sleeping accommodations we have."

While George rarely accompanies Celeste to her children's homes for babysitting, he welcomes all of the grandchildren to the cottage and to their winter residence in Mexico. And Celeste is happy to accommodate George's grandchildren. In fact, she and George's oldest grandson have a tradition every summer when they go rock climbing together.

Sam and Geraldine have a different, perhaps less stressful routine with grandchildren. For Sam, it's a second marriage, but for Geraldine, it's her first marriage. "Neither my sister nor I had married or had children," she explains, "so for me, having Sam's grandchildren is really special. As far as I'm concerned, they're my grandchildren. And for my mother, they're special too, since she never had grandchildren."

When they babysit Sam's grandchildren, they both participate. Geraldine, a former teacher, is right there to help the kids with homework and of course, to make sure they eat healthy meals and practice good manners.

Of course, there is also the challenge of not stepping on the rights of the 'other grandparents,' the birth grandparents. A 'step-grandparent' needs to use diplomacy in playing the role and know when to step back. Duncan and Liz have 12 grandchildren, with 10 of them belonging to Liz's children and two of them belonging to Duncan's son. As far as Liz is concerned, Duncan's grandchildren are her responsibility, since Duncan's first wife died 10 years ago. But Liz's first husband, the grandfather to her 10 grandchildren takes a very active role, so "Duncan knows when to step back and defer to him," Liz says.

The children of remarried parents are very much aware of 'fairness,' when it comes to time and effort spent on grandchildren. When Lloyd joined his second wife, Brenda one Saturday night to babysit her grandchildren, he did so with a proviso: "Don't tell my daughter I did this," he cautioned Brenda. While he didn't make a practice of babysitting for his grandchildren, he didn't want his daughter to think he was being unfair by helping Brenda babysit hers.

25.WELCOMING A STEP GRANDCHILD

With more than one-third of all marriages ending in divorce before the 30th wedding anniversary, many grandparents have become step-grandparents when a grown child remarries someone with children.

For Anna, becoming a step-grandmother was a happy event. She had neither married nor had children of her own when, at the age of 59, she married Wesley. Wesley was divorced, with four children and six grandchildren. "I know I'm not their biological grandmother," Anna says, "but I am delighted with the experience of having these little people in my life and being able to do activities with them that I've never done before."

For other grandparents, the complexities of new blended families are not as straightforward. It's often a difficult transition, especially for children whose world has completely changed, with new members of an extended family, often all strangers. The transition can be almost as disconcerting for a generation who thought their children and grandchildren would live happily ever after.

While some divorces may be quite civilized and amicable, there is still a period of adjustment and acceptance for everyone involved. The next hurdle is to use the same skills to accept a new blended family when a grown child remarries and brings a new spouse and children to the family gathering. It's unrealistic to expect there will be no bitterness or anxiety among the major players when a family structure changes. You may have just gotten through supporting a grown daughter in a divorce as well as your own sense of loss at the absence of a son-in-law you really loved when your daughter brings home a new partner with children of his own.

Where do grandparents fit in this new blended family?

The first rule is to realize that a step family is different. A new grandchild who is not part of your biological family knows she is different. She is struggling to be part of a new family, which may include step siblings, a new step mom or dad as well as a new set of step grandparents. She will be looking for equality with her new siblings, your natural grandchildren.

Polish up your sensitivity for this new grandchild. You may never love her the way you love the grandkids you already have, but you can respect her and be sensitive to her change in status. She's not the one who fell in love with someone new and decided to merge with another family.

Be prepared for rejection, even once you're learned to love a new grandchild. Instant love doesn't happen in step families, especially with older children. If you enjoy children, it's a chance to help a new grandchild through a difficult transition.

Being the most supportive grandparent means treating all grandchildren equally. That's difficult enough with biological families, but with step-grandchildren, it's challenging for some. Family psychologist Dr. R.C. Dubuc recommends treating step grandchildren with the same consideration as biological grandkids in terms of gifts, praise and time spent together. Of course, each child is an individual and if one grandson loves hockey, while a step grandson is more interested in books, it makes sense to honor those interests with different gifts, not two hockey sticks. But generally, children want to be treated with respect and with the same fairness given to their counterparts in the family. Recognizing their interests will make them feel they are valued.

"We make sure we give all the grandchildren gifts of equal value for birthdays," says Raymond. "but I draw the line at inheritances. My step grandkids have their own grandparents to look after leaving them money in their wills." Most step grandchildren, by a certain age, will be able to understand estate planning and that they are not being treated unfairly.

26.RAISING A CHILD---AGAIN?

When Nancy's teenage daughter decided to have her baby, Nancy offered to raise the child as her own. That was back in the late 50s when her decision to raise her grandson was a common solution to teen pregnancies.

Surprisingly since then, the numbers of grandparents raising their grandchildren has more than doubled. Why is this happening? Aren't we done with raising our family?

Besides teen pregnancy, child abuse, divorce, job loss, incarceration and illness, especially HIV/AIDS all contribute to the reasons the numbers of grandparents parenting their grandchildren have increased. Another common reason is substance abuse by the child's parent. When child welfare authorities step in, they make an attempt to keep the child in the family fold---hence the grandparents stepping up to the plate.

The good news is that, in what is being dubbed 'the skip generation,' these children do as well or better than kids in two-parent, biological families in terms of health and behavior.

That's encouraging for a generation of kids who might otherwise end up on the street or worse. But few of us plan to raise a second family and there are considerably more challenges than we faced raising our own.

First of all, we're facing our own mortality and worry about who will care for these kids when we're gone. And let's face it, many of us are susceptible to age-related diseases that, at the very least, affect our physical energy and emotional stamina in being responsible for children who require care 24/7. When Nancy faced the challenge of raising her grandson back in the 50s, she was in her early 40s. Grandparents who are 20-30 years older than Anna may not enjoy the same vigor.

Here are some strategies for coping with your new parenting role:

Create a secure home. Let your grandchildren know they are welcome and safe. Set up a daily routine with clear rules and discipline that rewards good behavior with praise. Dr. Staci Illsley, a Vancouver psychologist, specializing in children and adolescents, says the quality of the relationship and the secure attachment to a family member is important. "A child needs to know you're here when she needs you," she says.

Find activities to share. Finding common interests will help nurture this new relationship and make children feel involved in their new home. Get computer savvy and find activities that will keep both of you healthy and reduce stress too. Children of all ages will love to plant a garden in the spring. For older kids, find books and music you *both* like. Younger children appreciate the consistency of having a story read at bedtime.

Expect involvement. Children thrive when they feel involved. And you can use the help. Even a five-year-old can set the table. Teens can learn to do their own laundry. Small tasks teach responsibility and give them a stake in their own sense of security in your home.

Take care of yourself. If you are feeling stressed, it will translate to your grandchild. And it will affect your health. Talk to your doctor about your new responsibilities and get her input. Find a friend or family member who will take over regularly to give you a break. Step up your fitness level and sense of well being with yoga or a meditation class. Laugh often.

Find support. Feeling isolated is common for grandparents raising a family. Talk regularly to a friend, a professional or another grandparent in the same situation. Check out support groups and your library for parenting books. You'll get some good ideas and reassurance that you're doing a great job.

27. SUPPORT FOR SINGLE PARENT GRANDCHILDREN

Being a single parent is such hard work. A solo mom or dad is on call 24/7, as primary cook, caregiver, disciplinarian, nurse, confidante, driver/escort and homework buddy. There is no respite. And, for single dads of girls or moms of boys, there's the added job of figuring out how to put on hockey gear and ballet tutus, not to mention reassurance and advice about body changes, sex and other rites of passage.

Besides a double workload, a single parent can suffer from feeling lonely and overwhelmed unless a support system is in place. Certainly joint custody, the norm in many divorces these days, offers some guarantee of stability, predictability and even respite, but there are many single-parent families who don't enjoy that civilized kind of sharing. That's where grandparents can play a very important role.

When Kristen decided to adopt a baby girl on her own, she had lots of conversations with her parents before proceeding with the adoption. "I knew I was going out on a limb," she admits, "so it was really important that my parents were on board with my idea and were willing to help out and be my major support system."

Her dad, Frank says "We were certainly concerned about Kristen taking on such a huge responsibility, but we also knew she had maturity and the right attitude. She had a very realistic plan for handling parenthood on her own," he says. "Since we live a few blocks away, we were happy to make a commitment to help her out when she needed support."

While parenting can be full of surprises, Kristen and her parents felt it was important to set up a routine so everyone knew what to expect. Stability is important to young children and Frank and Elsie wanted some predictability in their role as grandparents too. "We set up a schedule so that we picked up the baby from daycare two evenings a week so Kristen could work late, see a movie with friends or run errands," says Elsie. "Now our grand-daughter is in kindergarten and we still have the same routine, where we pick her up, take her to the playground and home for dinner."

Giving a single parent a break is critical to her well being and also a chance for the grandchildren to bond with their grandparents. A single parent appreciates knowing she can count on that break. And for children, the stability of a regular, predictable date with grandparents is important too. Setting up a routine on a regular basis works for everyone.

However, it's equally important for grandparents not to take on more than they can handle. Be realistic about your own capabilities and health when making a commitment. It's better to commit to an hour of babysitting once a week than to promise a sleepover or full day of babysitting that may compromise your health.

Support your single-parent child without taking over. As tempting as it is to take on the role of the missing parent, don't try to fill those shoes.

Your job as a grandparent has its own special worth. For instance, a grandfather can provide a good male role model, as long as the role model doesn't infringe on the disciplinary rules and values of the single parent. A single mom needs to know she can count on your support of her values too. Respect the household rules so your grandchildren get a consistent message from all the adults in their lives.

Foster a healthy attitude to the family unit. Whether a single-parent family has been created out of divorce or death or by choice, it should be respected as valuable entity. A single-parent family, conscientiously cared for, is no more 'broken' or 'fractured' than a two-parent family where there is constant conflict or abuse.

It takes courage to be a solo parent with all the multi-tasking. Don't forget to praise your single-parent child for the great job he or she is doing.

28. GRANDPARENTS ON NANNY DUTY

R ebecca, 56 is the caregiver for her two grandsons five days a week. "My daughter drops them off every morning," she explains. "I enjoy taking care of them and it helps my daughter and her husband defray the costs of child care."

There are lots of reasons besides the cost of a daycare centre or a live-in nanny for choosing a grandparent as the caregiver. Finding a recommended daycare centre close to home or work is the first challenge. Secondly, daycare centers have a schedule to keep and may close before a parent finishes the workday.

A live-in (or out) nanny may have more flexible hours, making it easier to schedule play dates or appointments for children, but can be expensive enough that the second income in the family is hardly worth the cost.

And then, there's the issue of trust. Despite intensive interviews and reference checks, a daycare centre or a nanny means entrusting the care of a child to strangers.

So for many working couples, the ideal solution is to have someone who knows the child, can be trusted and best of all, loves the child unconditionally. That's grandma and often, her sidekick, grandpa.

Of course, there are considerations before taking on the job. And it is a job, albeit one that keeps us stimulated, active and engaged. But a grandparent as nanny has to be prepared to give up certain aspects of retirement such as sleeping in or finishing that great book, daytime bridge or going to a spur-of-the-moment afternoon movie.

Health issues are a factor to consider realistically. While a grown child may think his parents have the same energy they had 30 years ago, only you, as the prospective caregiver can honestly assess –and admit--your physical and emotional capabilities.

Martha and David took on the care of their one-year-old grandson, Elliott when his mom returned to work after maternity leave. "We did it happily for six months and then David's mother had a fall," says Martha, who has osteoarthritis. "Now, he's gone most of the day taking care of her needs and I find caring for Elliott on my own really tiring."

Because no one can foresee unexpected events, it's good to have a backup plan for childcare, or better still, an opportunity for respite for the fulltime grandparent/caregiver.

"The boys both goes to a playgroup two afternoons a week," says Rebecca, "and I cherish that downtime to be able to rest or enjoy activities of my own."

Will you be paid? "I wouldn't think of it," scoffs Rebecca. But Martha and David disagree. "While we don't expect a salary, we expect Elliott's parents to cover everyday costs such as special foods and outings."

While grandparents tend to overindulge grandchildren, it may not work on a daily basis –for the child or the grandparent. But, parents should allow grandparents some latitude too so they don't feel they are being micro-managed in the job.

Not only have parenting philosophies changed since we were parents, but safety regulations have too with everything from crib standards to bike helmets and toy labeling. Keep a list of emergency numbers, including the poison control centre and figure out a fire drill procedure for your home.

With realistic expectations and preparedness, being the caregiver gives a grandparent the opportunity to stay young, stimulated and involved and to mold a grandchild in the *perfect* image of oneself.

29.INDULGING PICKY EATERS

Most of us came from an era where we were told "to eat everything on our plate...or else." I don't recall what "or else" meant, but I do remember another phrase used that made no sense to me. The reasoning my parents used was "there are children starving in China." My logical answer as a child to that was: Then, send them my dinner!

Children today have far more freedom to be choosy about what they eat. And, with a wide range of pre-packaged, ready- to- serve foods available, there's very little need to make meals from scratch from those basic healthy ingredients that were part of our diet as children. Even carrot sticks come in small, peeled, washed, bite-sized chunks now. Cheese doesn't need to be sliced from a block. It comes pre-packaged as cheese strings. And then there's the array of junk food, bags of chocolate-infused cookies, fruit rollups and gushers, even little packs of crackers with yellow-orange gunk proclaiming to be cheese.

In a week spent cooking dinners and packing school lunches for my grandsons, I realized how vast the network of food choices is. I also realized that most kids today, including my grandsons, are the decision makers in terms of what they will eat. Each of my grandsons has a favorite dinner, all completely different and they have definite ideas about what goes into their packed lunches. Finley, at eight loves everything. Hudson, at 13, needs to have his food separated on the plate. Finley will eat sushi, salads, roast beef (with horseradish, please) and his favorite meal is pickerel. Hudson's favorite meal is spaghetti and meatballs, but the meatballs must be in a separate pile on his plate from the spaghetti. If it's pasta night, Jack, 15, prefers it with chicken and Alfredo sauce.

For the first few days, I placed myself under enormous pressure to please each of them, especially since I was taking over for their regular nanny, who according to them "cooked gross stuff!" Charged with a challenge, I made different meals for all three for the first two nights. I drove myself crazy and the kitchen had turned into a full-service deli with me as the short-order cook. My daughter put an end to that very quickly and told me to make one meal of my choice and serve it to them. End of discussion. So the third night, I made a stir-fry to work some vegetables into their diet. And yes, I still separated Hudson's meat into a pile and each kind of vegetable into a mound. He ate it, but wasn't really overjoyed. I had to resign myself to accepting the fact that I cannot please all three of them all the time.

Can we blame the parents for letting children rule when it comes to food choices? Perhaps in some cases, but my daughter is adamant that they eat what is prepared and learn to try new foods. So while we can all surmise that working parents indulge children with the foods they love because the parents feel guilty or are just too tired at the end of the day to argue, I have to admit I am just as guilty or more so. Food has always been my way of showing love, and that seems to translate into pleasing people with what they prefer to eat.

Pickiness may be a tradition handed down too. If a parent is picky, a child will imitate. Millie and Don find their grand-daughter's eating habits frustrating. "She is very picky and will absolutely not try new things," Millie explains. "We couldn't understand until one Sunday dinner when our daughter-in-law, turned her nose up at the salmon we were serving. It was easy to see where Chloe had developed the picky habit."

With childhood obesity, stemming from super-sized fast food as well as other culprits, a serious problem in North America, we need to return to the sanity of 'real food' prepared according to nutritional guidelines. The bottom line is we, the grandparents, and of course, the parents, need to be in charge of the food choices, not the kids.

I'm a bit nervous about opening their lunchboxes when they come home from school today to see what's still there uneaten. I'll just have to try harder for tomorrow's lunches.

The Joys of Grandparenting

30. THE GIFTS WE BUY FOR GRANDKIDS

A grandmother is not a fairy godmother and grandpa is definitely not Santa. Depending on income, gifts to grandchildren can range from small gifts from the dollar store to registered education contributions. The gift also determines who it's important to make smile--- your child or grandchild.

The truth is that in a society where excess seems rampant, especially with toys, electronics and riding vehicles, it's getting tough for grandparents to make an impression. Whether you're funding your grandchild's education or simply looking for that birthday smile, there are some guidelines about gifts that grandparents agree are important.

First of all, check with the child's parents about appropriateness. Dorothy, a first-time grandmother says "I wouldn't buy toys with finding out what my son and daughter-in-law suggest. They research everything for the baby, so they know what is the safest, what is best."

Secondly, fair doesn't always mean equal. Mary Beth puts money into a college savings plan for her three grandchildren. The younger daughter felt her one child should receive the same amount as the combined amount for her sister's two children. "It caused hard feelings," admits Mary Beth, "but for me, I can only afford a certain amount, so to double the amount for my younger daughter's child was not in my budget."

The question of fairness revolves around whether you give the same amount to each family or to each child. The decision is up to you.

Jonathon and Addie gave each of their seven grandchildren $5000 as part of the deposit on a house when they were ready to buy a new home. "We made the decision to give the same amount to each grandchild, even though four of our grandchildren are the children of one of our kids," says Jonathon. "Our other children never suggested it wasn't fair."

Then there are the tangible gifts that can be nothing short of overload for the child, and most especially for the grandparents' budget. Toys and gadgets at all age levels abound in variety with prices to match. While I still believe toddlers have as much fun with pots, lids and wooden spoons, today's parents want the latest and greatest for their precious babes. And, as kids get older, they expect to have their own phones as well as all forms of riding vehicles, scooters and skateboards.

From the time my grandkids were babies, I derived great pleasure from shopping for clothes. It was much more fun for me than for them. Now that Jack is 15, he likes clothes, so my passion is finally rewarded. Like most grandparents, I believe it's the parents' responsibilities to buy the big gifts: the first two-wheeler, the dollhouse, the iPod.

Lastly, gifts from grandparents don't have to cost the whole month's grocery money. A gift can be as simple---and old-fashioned--- as a special book that was their dad's when he was a kid or a birdhouse they can hang in the backyard. Older grandchildren appreciate a family heirloom you've been keeping just for them.

If there's a birthday coming up for your school-aged grandchild, with the parents' approval, surprise her at school and take her out for lunch at her favorite fast-food place. Small gestures are often the most meaningful.

31.ENTITLEMENT: IT'S ALL ABOUT SHOES

After spending a week in Kenya with *Free the Children*, I think one of my most lasting impressions was the difference between Kenyan children and North American children in what they have and their *attitudes* to what they have.

At the schools in the Maasai Mara, children are often in bare feet. Families cannot afford shoes for all the children. They do have school uniforms: white shirts, blue, green or red sweaters depending on the school and short pants for boys, skirts for girls. Although their school uniforms are clean and neat, I noticed many had holes in the underarms of their sweaters. Some of them walk one or two hours to get to school every day, through a savannah that may have zebras or life-threatening lions or elephants. While elementary school is compulsory, high school requires tuition, an impossible dream for most kids, especially girls, who are often married off at the age of thirteen to become one of several wives to a man who may be old enough to be their father.

Free the Children has built more than 100 schools in Kenya providing education to more than 7,000 children every day, including a boarding school for secondary school girls. For all of these children, the opportunity to go to school, instead of hauling 20-litre jugs of water from a muddy river, fetching firewood, herding goats or caring for younger children, is a gift that makes their eyes shine with sheer joy and appreciation, and their dreams of breaking the chain of poverty a potential reality.

Fast forward to North America a week later, where many of our grandkids are bused to school. No wonder we have a problem with obesity. They have closets clogged with different shoes for every sport, not to mention 'indoor' and 'outdoor' shoes for school. It doesn't matter whether their clothes come from Old Navy or Abercrombie and Fitch; they have lots of clothes. They also have cell phones and iPods as soon as they're old enough to punch in numbers or send a text. Many of our grandchildren feign tummy aches or any variety of illness to get out of going to school. They certainly do not have that bright-eyed enthusiasm I saw in Kenya.

When they get home from school, apart from having to do homework, our grandkids can play video or computer games, watch something on high definition television, play with friends or raid the fridge for snacks. "There's nothing to eat," is a familiar refrain. Check out Africa, kids! There often really is nothing to eat, unless you cook something over a wood fire and there is certainly no fridge full of snacks.

After seeing the work *Free the Children* is doing in Kenya, I feel hope and optimism for those children. With education, clean water, sanitation, health care and lessons in micro finance for the women, the children have a chance at a bright future, while developing their own incentives, using the valuable ideals of their culture and becoming self-sustaining, responsible citizens.

Not sure I have the same optimism for our grandchildren. It's not their fault of course. The media charms them with the gadgets and electronics they should have. Busy parents give too much to assuage the guilt from being at work long hours. Teen grandkids boast about the coolest gadgets, Disney vacations and the most friends on Facebook.

Unfortunately, this sense of entitlement grandkids have diminishes their incentive, their creativity and any pride of ownership. Why should they? They made no sacrifices or effort to get the rows of hoodies or pretty dresses in their closet.

We're not doing them any favors in the long run. The secret to stopping a sense of entitlement is to give kids a sense of ownership and responsibility for buying their own stuff. They need jobs around the house for which they get paid. Their earned money gives them the chance to own what they buy, appreciate the work they did to get their stuff and develop a sense of responsibility, maybe even resourcefulness.

Free the Children is working to rescue Kenyan children from poverty with basics we take for granted, give them a chance to thrive, use their ingrained sense of resourcefulness and make sensible choices for a sustainable future. As grandparents, we need to rescue our grandchildren from another kind of poverty: entitlement -- the kind of poverty that robs them of their real self worth and ingenuity.

32.SPECIAL GRANDCHILDREN WITH SPECIAL NEEDS

Susan's grandson has a mild intellectual disability, so when she received a story he had written about lions for school in the mail, she called him to tell him how nice it was to get 'good mail' and how much she liked his story. He reminded her that he didn't get good mail either, and it would be nice if she could write him back. Having letters to read is good practice for him and Susan has the time to write them. It's an easy way for her to help out.

When children have special needs, the onus on their parents is more time-consuming and intense. While grandparents don't have the day-to-day responsibilities, we can be supportive to the parents and arm ourselves with the information we need to know about the specific condition. Dr. Staci Illsley, a Vancouver psychologist who specializes in children and adolescents suggests that "grandparents educate themselves in a general sense to what their grandchild may be going through" and recommends further that "grandparents can play a special role in taking kids away from the daily grind and engaging them in fun activities."

When his three-year-old grand-daughter, Laura, was diagnosed with juvenile arthritis (JIA), Malcolm's reaction was "this doesn't happen in our family." Were we healthier in previous generations or did some conditions simply not get diagnosed? Whatever the answer, Malcolm says his role is to support Laura's mom, his daughter, Heather. "My heart was bleeding for her in the beginning," he says, "so I tried to keep her optimistic and offer support in a cheerleading kind of way." Laura is now being monitored and for the most part, enjoys all the normal activities of a three-year-old. "Once Heather saw other kids with JIA at the hospital, who were living normal lives, she felt better," Malcolm says.

Lyn and Byron have an eight-year-old grand-daughter who has tuberous sclerosis, a genetic disease that causes benign tumors to form in major organs. When Cate was diagnosed shortly after birth, Lyn and Byron were apprehensive. "It was like a kick in the stomach," Lyn says, "but as time went on, the baby thrived and we passed the critical milestones the doctors gave us. We were able to take a deep breath and say 'it's going to be okay.' There are still milestones, but the older she gets, the risks are less critical." Today, while Cate and her teachers know she must take certain precautions such as keeping a water bottle at hand, she is involved in dance, skating and swimming and other activities young girls enjoy. "As a grandparent, I can say she's the most normal kid on the block," Lyn says, "and that's the way we treat her."

When a child is born with special needs, it impacts on all members of the family. At first, there may be denial and grief that your grandchild isn't perfect. But the next important emotional step is acceptance because every child is special with his own brand of unique joy. For resources check out the library for books such as Understanding Your Special-Needs Grandchild by Clare B Jones or Grandparenting a Child with Special Needs by Charlotte Thompson (Parentbooks).

33.FIVE FORBIDDEN STATEMENTS FOR GRANDPARENTS

I f only our children would raise our grandkids using our advice. After all, we did a fine job, for the most part. Sometimes they do ask for advice. Rarely, but it does happen.

The tough challenge for grandparents is to refrain from giving advice when it isn't invited. It's a natural instinct to tell our children what they should and should not do. We've been doing it all their lives, after all.

But parenting styles and values are very different today from ours. Most young parents do their research and develop their own parenting styles based more on what the "experts" and their friends are suggesting. We, the grandparents are on the periphery of the advisory circle.

It's fair that they want to raise their children their way. More than that, they want our approval and pride in their decisions about their children. It took me many years as a grandparent to get that message and to keep my opinions to myself, unless asked.

Here are some common things even the best-intentioned grandparents say. Trust me, they are fighting words!

1. **When you were a child...** Follow that with any anecdote you like, whether it's bedtime rituals, breakfast cereal or childhood illnesses, what you are really saying is "you're doing it wrong. Here's how it should be done." Try to remove this statement from your small-talk repertoire, unless you preface it with something more helpful such as "I understand what you're going through."

2. **I think you should name the baby...** It doesn't matter whether you come up with a name or think they should name her after

Aunt Brenda, it's not your right or responsibility to name the baby.

3. **Relax, don't worry about it.** Sometimes, our children just want to vent their frustrations and have someone listen--- and who better than a mom or dad. They don't want advice and they really don't want to be told to relax. They take parenting responsibilities seriously and what may seem a minor problem to you isn't necessarily minor to them.

4. **I'm expecting all of you for Thanksgiving.** Or Easter, Christmas, Hanukkah, even Church on Sunday. Your child now has a spouse with parents who may have the same notion. Don't put them in a position of having to choose. As a family on their own, they need to negotiate their plans themselves. Everyone has heard of young families spending most of Christmas Day on the road between grandparents' houses. What fun is that for anyone?

5. **Do you really think you should let him do that?** Let's face it. That is not a question. It's a criticism. Unless your grandchild is about to embark on an act that may endanger his safety or shove the scissors down the dog's throat, remain mute.

The most challenging aspect of being a grandparent is refraining from giving an opinion or advice, unless it's asked for specifically. Tough to do, when we're such experts. However, commending the work they're doing as parents will go much further in showing you care and respect them as the adults you did such a good job of raising.

34. THOSE OTHER GRANDPARENTS

When our grown children marry, we are challenged with new personalities and new people to love. Our new son-in-law or daughter- in- law also brings his or her own set of parents, but once the wedding is over, we don't usually have to impress them anymore. Then the grandchildren come along. The challenge of loving the kids is easy, of course. But those other grandparents seem to be back in the picture and more visible and involved than we'd like. In an ideal world, we'd have exclusive access to our grandchildren.

The fact is, the kids are their grandchildren too, so we do have to share the joy. It means traditional holidays and family get-togethers have to be negotiated and shared. No more exclusive rights to Christmas, Passover and Mother's Day. We either share or accept alternating holidays with those other grandparents.

Whether it's fair or not, it seems that the girl's family gets first rights and first refusal when it comes to all events surrounding grandchildren. That includes presence at the birth, babysitting and special occasions. There is, at work, that mother-daughter bond and perhaps it's just natural that a young mother is going to look to the comfort and familiarity of her own mother when she needs advice and help with her child.

As much as we can intellectualize the reasons and previous bonds that exist, it can still be hurtful to the grandmother who is left out of those intimate situations with a new grandchild.

Unfortunately, too, in many cases, a mother-in-law , who a new bride has challenged for control already has points scored against her, so adding grandchildren to the relationship is not likely going to transform it into a trusting friendship. Margaret Mead once wrote: "Of all the peoples whom I have studied, from city dwellers to cliff dwellers, I always find that at least 50 per cent would prefer to have at least one jungle between themselves and their mothers-in-law."

Each set of grandparents comes with its own peculiar values and attitudes too. While one set may lavish a child with toys and gifts, another set of grandparents may believe strongly in not catering to all the toys and gadgets a child may want. It can cause resentment, obviously, when a child favors the grandparents who always come bearing gifts. The truth is, overindulgence is never a healthy for a child and the child's parents will, hopefully, set out guidelines to prevent it. Besides, children live in the moment, so if one grandma has arrived with a trunk full of just-what-I-wanted toys, chances are all will be forgotten in a day or two and the other grandma will regain her rightful place of favor. As long as a grandchild feels secure in our relationship, it won't matter who brought the new doll stroller.

Competition and jealousy aside, from the grandchild's perspective, the more grandparents they have to shower them with love and praise, the more secure they will feel.

35. THE SOCIALIZATION OF GRANDCHILDREN

One night over dinner, my grandsons were discussing the comparable merits of Michael Jackson and Justin Bieber. Eight-year-old Finley is enchanted with Michael Jackson, can do the moonwalk and various other MJ moves (although his mother has told him that grabbing his crotch is not appropriate behavior). When Finley announced that everyone in his grade one class hates Justin Bieber, his older brothers chastised him severely and when they said "how would you like it if we said we hate Michael Jackson," Finley dissolved in tears.

Later, I explained to him that hate was a strong word for his classmates to use, especially for someone they didn't know, and that he should really 'be his own person' and not agree with their assessment, if he didn't want to. His response was "but Grammie, I just want to fit in."

I had to admit his reason for going along with the class pronouncement, while not particularly positive, was a valid rationale for a six-year-old, who has begun the process of socialization, where having the same opinion is important. Being different doesn't cut it with six year olds.

Ah for the days when he was a baby and socialization was not a priority. Babies are born with no culture and we as parents, grandparents and teachers instruct them in the mores of being socially adept.

Socialization varies from culture to culture and children mimic the values of their particular society as well as those of the individual parents. In our North American society, when a baby cries for no physical reason, we tend to soothe and cajole until the crying stops. However, in the Navajo culture, the same baby is removed from the social milieu and isolated until the crying ends, then is rewarded with a return to the group. The Navajo child learns that crying is not appropriate social behavior whereas our babies learn that crying results in more social contact.

Finley has also learned that he can 'fit in' by being generous with his friends. A girl in his class was envious of Finley's sea monkeys, so he asked me to buy the girl some too. I did, but then a boy in his class asked for some. Despite my explanation that the boy's parents should buy sea monkeys for him, Finley was upset because he had "promised to get them." Yes, my mistake was buying them for the first friend!

Socialization has an ugly side too. Bullying seems to be rampant in schools these days. Ian and Janice have two grandchildren who have both been bullied. "Our oldest grand-daughter, at 15 is a really good athlete and gets on the senior teams, which means other senior girls are bumped off," explains Ian. "The rejected girls were overheard planning to 'beat up Melissa Archer' and the school had to call in special hall monitors to keep an eye out for any confrontation." Their 12-year-old grandson has ADHD and also often gets bullied in the playground for acting inappropriately and not 'fitting in.'

Stuart and Caroline were appalled when their 12-year-old grandson was called to the principal's office. A 14-year-old girl and her buddies had been chasing him at recess. " Scott assumed the girl really liked him and started writing little notes to her, telling her he thought she was beautiful," Stuart explains. "The girl complained to the office, and Scott was reprimanded for sending the notes and told to stop. What really annoys us, is that the girl was actually being a bully and giving Scott the wrong impression, but he's the one who was humiliated by the situation. And the school took no responsibility for her part in the harassment."

Was it always this difficult and complicated when we were children or when our own kids were growing up? While we know that eventually, children grow up to be individuals with their own brand of personality and are even encouraged and rewarded socially when they're different and stand out, it takes patience to wait out this period of fitting into the same pattern of behavior.

And as a society, we need to stop the bullying. Maybe it's up to us grandparents to do something about it.

36.WHY MUST GRANDKIDS BE SO HONEST?

My eight-year-old grandson, Finley drew a picture of the two of us last week and carefully slid it into a frame for me to keep. I complimented his art work, of course, but did ask him about the squiggly lines on my legs. "That's the hair on your legs, grammie," he replied matter-of-factly. He's either too observant or much too honest. Whichever is the case, I realized it was time for a waxing appointment.

A grandparent generally needs to relinquish any personal sensitivity once a grandchild can talk and observe things such as age spots, wrinkles, grey roots and protruding tummies or upper-arm jiggles. Their wide-eyed honesty can be somewhat brutal. I've changed my hair color after my grandsons referred to me as "grammie with the orange hair," and one of their grandpas wonders why they call him "big-tummy grandpa" when their other grandpa, who is called "skinny grandpa" really isn't all that skinny.

Once we get beyond the sensitive side of this brand of honesty, the comments can be useful in making some lifestyle changes we should have made in the first place, particularly if it means more exercise and a healthier daily routine.

The honesty of grandchildren can also be effective in reminding us of the little white lies we probably tell every day. One summer, I decided to take Finley to a cooking class for children aged 7 to 12. He wouldn't be seven for another few months, but he's tall for his age and of course, very, very smart, so I thought we could slide by the age rule with some justification. His dad and I had both told him that if asked, he should just say that he is seven. But just before we were ready to drive to the class, he confided his reticence to going along with our plan to me: "Grammie, it would be a bad lie to say I am seven."

Not only did I feel appropriately chastised, but I was also embarrassed that this little boy now knew that not only his perfect dad but also his perfect grammie was fallible. After all, one of the joys of grand parenting is that we finally have little people who adore us and believe we are perfect. It's been a long time since their parents, our children felt the same way.

I had to agree with him that telling a lie was wrong. We agreed that we would say he was "almost seven." It turned out the cooking class was cancelled, so the age dilemma was never addressed. But the incident has made me more aware of the importance of values such as honesty and our role as grandparents in fostering those standards of behavior.

Honesty is an important value that children need to learn in order to develop into adults who are trustworthy. While Fin will soon need to learn that some forms of honesty that hurt feelings need to be avoided or simply not voiced, for now, I will encourage and praise most of his forthright comments.

37. GRANDCHILDREN ALLOW US TO LIVE IN THE MOMENT

Rita had just spent a week looking after her two grandchildren both under the age of six. She was exhausted, but confided to a group of friends that the up side of the experience was that she could "live in the moment of the kids' lives, their needs and antics." For a week, Rita had absolutely no time to worry about anything else.

Let's be honest. The golden years sometimes have a tarnished patina. Some of the same stresses and worries that followed us during our years of working and raising a family continue to plague us. There are financial concerns about supporting our later years and worries about our health and managing age-related illnesses. Rita's 90-year-old mother was also a major concern for her on a daily basis.The magic times spent with grandkids dispels, albeit temporarily, those concerns. We get to forget while we are drawn into living in the moment.

I spent 11 weeks with my three grandsons last year. At the end of every day, after sending them off to school with a good breakfast and a packed lunch, I tackled laundry and meal preparation. When they arrived home, there was homework, snacks, after-school activities and dinner to prepare and clean up afterwards. By the time everyone was bathed and pajama-ed, I fell into bed, sometimes before them. For 11 weeks, I had no age-plagued sleeplessness. In fact, not only did I sleep soundly, I lost eight pounds and felt muscles I forgot I had—probably from running up and down stairs, chasing the puppy out of flowerbeds and running alongside my six-year-old grandson as he biked up and down hills.

There was no time to worry about money, health or any other concerns. While I don't want to take on the fulltime job of looking after three busy boys, this temporary stint gave me a sense of purpose, a feeling that I could contribute to the family life of my daughter and son-in-law.

 My eight-year-old grandson, with his fascination about the fact that I am "very old," told me one night as he snaked his little arm around my waist that he wished I were one year old. When I asked why, he replied "because then you would live forever."

After a Tae Kwon Do class with my 13-year-old grandson, I raved about how well he had done. His response was "I did it all for you, Grammie."

When my oldest grandson celebrated his 15th birthday, he and I went for dinner at his favorite restaurant. He commented on the way that "this will be our restaurant, Grammie." I know it won't be long until I am way down the list of his favorite dinner companions, but for now, that sentiment about our bond warms my heart.

These magic moments, the ones our grandchildren offer us the opportunity to live in, soften the sometimes harsh challenges of aging. They're useful memories to relive and cherish on sleepless nights.

The Joys of Grandparenting

ABOUT THE AUTHOR

Bonnie Baker Cowan is a writer, editor and author with more than 35 years experience as a journalist. A former editor in chief of Canadian Living and 50Plus magazines, she is currently a freelance writer and editor, with a regular grand parenting column in Zoomer magazine. She lives in Toronto and a 35-minute drive from her three grandsons. Their mom and dad are happy to let her share the pleasure of their children's company. She's waiting for her other two children to bless her with more grandchildren.

Made in the USA
Lexington, KY
05 June 2013